MW01241789

Published by TJS Publishing House
PO BOX 2382
Matthews, NC 28106
www.tjspublishinghouse.com

Published in the United States of America.

ISBN-13: 978-1-952833-36-6
ISBN-10: 1-952833-36-1

DEDICATION

I would like to dedicate this book to the woman who's afraid. To any woman that is afraid to speak up, to let go or release, to move forward or to be yourself. To the one who's afraid to shake things up a little. This book is for you.

I would also like to dedicate this book to my sister, Tamara and my oldest daughter, Aubrei.

Tamara, you are a jewel and we have been through some tough times separately and together. Our situations were always different but somewhat similar. I want to begin with speaking out and believing that no matter how hard healing or letting go may be, it is necessary at some point in your life. I

did this afraid. I jumped. I would love
for you to jump with me.

Aubrei, my sweet baby girl, because you are the
oldest you've endured more with me than the others.
I dedicate this book to you so you will know and
always know that Mommy will be okay. I want you to
see how brave and strong mommy is. You've seen a
lot, even down to the tears but this is dedicated to you
baby girl. Mommy jumped and I am on the road of
true and divine healing.

Afraid and all, I'm doing it.

ACKNOWLEDGMENTS

To my mother, Regina, thank you for being my number one supporter. Not just throughout the process of me writing this book for overall. Thank you being a shoulder to lean on. Listening to my ideas, hearing my heart and comforting me with your supportive words and prayers. Thank you for being he push that I needed to execute this book.

To my brother, Gary, thank you. I call you my "little big brother". Thank you for being here. Thank you for your support, your suggestions, your thoughts, your advice etc. thank you for being my brother. This was one the hardest things I've ever done. Thank you for pushing me and believing in me no matter what.

To my girl, Nisha, thank you for supporting me.
Thank you for allowing me to be in your space during
this time. I never understood why we crossed paths
but the one thing that pushed me towards finishing
what I had started, was the support and the words
you spoke into my life concerning my
healing process. I love you.

Lastly, my children. One day you will see me read
this book. Thank you for being amazing children. I
appreciate you guys for always stretching mommy,
challenging mommy, hugging mommy and
supporting mommy. You're going right now,
and you don't know what you're doing most
times but believe me, you are my reason.
All of you. Mommy loves you so much.

FOR NOW, IT'S JUST A BOOK.

This book is dedicated to you. Yes, you. The strong one. To the person that's the bigger person. To the one person, that's the yes person—the one with the big heart. Maybe misunderstood sometimes. I don't necessarily have to name every emotion or use lots of descriptive words because you know this book is for you.

I remember the exact day, time, and moment I picked up my laptop and began to type. I remember sitting on the couch, watching my newborn sleep his little life away. Wow, this child doesn't seem to care about anything in the world. As I stared at baby A'Prentice, I realized that the amount of trust this baby had in me to hold him, feed him, clothe him, nurture him, and love him, was nothing when compared to the amount of trust I had lacked within myself and, most importantly, God. I did not trust anything or anyone whatsoever. I didn't trust people because of past situations. I believed I deserved the selfish entitlement when I was disappointed in his decisions for my life. I am in love because of the lack of love I received as a child. In peace, because I have become immune to pain. I had no joy because I had the mentality that even if something literally made me happy, I subtly sabotaged those moments, waiting for some tragedy to happen. It hit me so hard in my chest that I began choking. I was holding back tears of disappointment and pain. The difference between this time and all the other times my light bulb came on was that instead of crying, instead of calling a friend or my mom to vent, get this... instead of praying, I picked up my laptop and began to type. No notes, only thoughts. For now, this is just a book, but *this* book…

TABLE OF CONTENTS

1

INNOCENCE

Where do I start? I am twenty-eight years old right now with three children. Aubrei is my oldest; she's ten years old. Aiyanna is my middle child, and she's seven years old. A'Prentice, my baby is six months old. I'm just typing, y'all. Let me start by saying this: I am FAR from innocent. I believe the situations that occurred during this week pushed me so close to the edge that I was afraid to do anything else but release. I am already feeling the weight being lifted. I didn't realize until a couple days ago that I never acknowledged the things that should have been years ago! I mean, this is the craziest sh*t ever. I literally held myself back for years, not even realizing that it was me until I hit a different rock bottom.

I'm not 100% sure what led me to name this chapter "Innocence." After all, I'm just typing. My thoughts are going; my mind is racing, and my fingers won't stop typing. When I think of the word innocent, I immediately think of a child. I often think of my childhood. I remember so many great memories of it, but I also vividly remember the very dark moments I experienced as a child. When a child's innocence is snatched away from them by emotional abuse, sexual abuse, physical abuse, or even mental abuse, the child is no longer innocent. This child is now attached to the very thing that snatched their innocence away.

Y'all, it's so deep... I am twenty-eight years old, and I realized two years ago that my childhood and childhood traumas had so much to do with the way I have been handling my precious life. Life is a beautiful thing, and we handle it recklessly. We take advantage of something that's been gifted to us. I am a woman whose innocence was snatched away at an early age. The disappointing part of realizing this is that I have operated out of anger, lust, bitterness, pain, and even self-doubt, all because I felt like something should've been given back to me.

Have you ever had something happen to you that made you feel like you absolutely did not deserve it? No, let's be real... We are undeserving of many things, and we thank the Lord for his grace and his mercy,

4

but what happens when that grace and mercy isn't enough for you to accept the fact that something HAPPENED— and you know for a fact that you didn't deserve it? What is your next move? Do you attempt to heal? Do you wait for an apology? Are you hoping for a magical experience that will completely remove your pain? I've done all those things and more, but the reality is that it happened.

It is a very dangerous thing to not only feel the pain and suffering from past hurtful situations, but to replay the trauma in your mind over and over again is even more dangerous. I was talking to a friend of mine a couple of days ago, and she asked me a question that I am just now able to respond to. She asked me, "Adrian, it happened to you, but have you acknowledged that it happened?" I began to stutter. "I mean, yeah, I've acknowledged it. I just don't talk about it... There was a pause. By this time, I could tell she was still waiting for me to really respond from my heart and give her an honest answer. "Well, okay, I've acknowledged it like I know it happened. I guess I just haven't accepted it yet. "There it was. I wanted to hang up that phone so badly. Accept it? Accept the fact that someone else bled on me as a child and took something from me? Hell no, I'm not accepting that because I didn't deserve it. No. I'm innocent. I was innocent!

I should not have to fight this thing off me daily because of someone else. Absolutely not! The anger I began feeling just from the thought of accepting something hurtful that had happened to me ached my heart. I thought about it for the rest of the day and into the next day. Isn't it just amazing how God works? I can't begin to describe how perfect and strategic he is. The only way I could be free from it all requires me to accept and release. Just wow! The moment I realized that was what I needed to do all along was the very moment I accepted and released it. I am releasing now, I thought, and it feels so good.

While staring at baby A'Prentice sleeping, I made the decision not to bring another child into my life while still wounded and bleeding from my past. It happened, and no, I didn't deserve it, but it happened, and it was time for me to be free, so I busted a move. Not only for my kids but for myself. I cannot type this and not be real with y'all. I love my children, and I strive for them daily, but I will not put pressure on myself that "no matter what, my kids will not deal with this or go through this." No, my reality was that I would never go through this again, that I would get my sh*t together and be able to enjoy this life WITH my children. Whole, healed and all.

My children will not go through the cycles I formed as an adult. That I can control, but the reality is, things happen. Things happen to good people, bad people, rich and poor people. We are indeed the children of God, and his covering over our lives doesn't guarantee skittles and rainbows. I could not control anything whatsoever as an innocent child, but this? My life now? My freedom? I can control what I decide to pour into my children's precious innocent lives. When you make the decision to take control of your life, you are teaching others how to treat and handle you because what you do with the limited time that's left in your life will pave the way for the rest of your life. Everything that we allow, everything that we tolerate, and everything that we attach ourselves to comes from the decisions we have made for ourselves. That's why it's essential to actually know who you are as an individual.

When you make the decision to take control of your life, you are teaching others how to treat and handle you because what you do with the limited time that's left in your life will pave the way for the rest of your life.

One thing I have learned and want to teach my children is how people forget to tell you that sometimes you'll find yourself feeling as if you have to trade your innocence for experience, but the truth is, deep inside, innocence will never die. Innocence is the pure key to happiness. Make the decision to accept, release, and be unapologetically happy. What you do with your innocence now is up to you.

What you do with your innocence now is up to you.

2

GUILT

It's obvious that once you begin to live your life freely, the sneaky monster of guilt approaches you at your front door. I handled guilt in a very unhealthy way. Now, as I begin to free myself, I am wondering why I always felt guilty about being happy. Why did I allow this guilt to dictate my happiness? After all, I am strong, right? So, I don't necessarily have to be happy, as long as I'm "okay." As long as my kids are taken care of, "I'm okay."

Guilt, the noun for guilty, is the fact of having committed a specified or implied offense or crime. As a verb, it is used to describe making someone feel guilty, especially in order to make them do something. I have given guilt too much of my life. I mean years of it. Not only do I feel guilty for being happy, but I also feel guilty for my mistakes. The feeling of owing someone or something because of a mistake you made is by far the most draining. Well, it was for me. I made so many mistakes. I'm certain I'll make more, but the stagnation of my growth came from me allowing my mistakes to define me.

So, when I made an honest mistake, I felt so horrible that I would do whatever it took to earn back friendships, relationships, and even the love of family members. Remember, this is just a book now, and I'm just typing. I made the mistake of labeling myself a mistake. Every thought, every move I made came from a place of hurt, and every time I felt like I had a grip on my life, I allowed it to slip right through my fingers. Do you ever think of being someone you've always needed as a child or even as an adult? I operated in that mode for so long that it began to consume me. Having a heart of gold has its blessings and curses. I can say now that no matter what I encounter, good or bad, I will remain who God has called me to be, which is a gracefully broken vessel that took her situation and turned it into something beautiful.

I am not doing this by starting a business, dressing up and having a night out with my girls to cover up my hurt, or taking a trip to get away, but I am dealing with this and releasing it all. Oh, I love God. I feel better already—just released. I deserve this. You deserve this. That sneaky monster that'll probably try to visit tomorrow morning WILL make you feel exactly what it's called; Guilty! But ask yourself, why? Why are you feeling this guilt? Did you make a mistake? Did you finally decide to live for God? Live for you? Are you feeling the guilt of leaving friends and family behind on your journey to happiness? Maybe the mistake you made with a friend or spouse haunts you into a space where you feel like you don't deserve that second chance. That's the one. That was the one for me.

I often found myself in isolation almost every other month. By all means, take the time you need to get yourself straight, but do not make it a habit. I formed an unhealthy isolation cycle that pushed away the most amazing people. My own children would suppress their feelings and emotions all because they knew mommy was in her "mood." "There I was, bleeding on my children." Teaching them one thing but living another. I mean, how chaotic was my house?

Not to mention, life itself tosses me from here to there. Guilt will rob you and take everything you've ever stood for from you. The thought of how far I could have been is not only disappointing but also relieving. Of course, everyone wishes they could travel back in time and make different decisions, but we can't.

I formed an unhealthy isolation cycle that pushed away the most amazing people.

We have to live for now and what we know now. I felt so much guilt after my husband died that I refused to accept anything less than the bare minimum from others. I made connections with people I knew weren't for me. I gave myself to people who did not deserve to have access to me in the first place. I became so accessible; I looked my past in the eyes and didn't even fight; neither did I show this past ghost that it was no longer welcome. Three years ago, to be exact, I decided to put myself back "on the map." I had made a decision to do so out of guilt. The difference between the guilt I felt for myself, and the guilt others believed I felt was the fact that I felt as if I didn't have enough time with my husband.

I felt like I should have been there more during his time of sickness. I should have been a better wife. I had labeled myself a mistake because of the mistakes I had made during my marriage. I became so angry after his death that I had absolutely no intentions of ever speaking to or about God anymore. I'll say this again: Isn't it mind-blowing the way God works? We get on our knees, and we pray daily for the things we want and desire, and just as soon as we don't get the answers we want or feel like we should get, we give up. We quit or become angry and bitter.

I prayed specifically for God to heal him. I was angry when he died. I think it's safe to say I was only able to release the fact that he was gone in 2021. Really? I released him, and I sat at his grave for over an hour. What's crazy about that is my ex-boyfriend had suggested we go. We took a beach trip, and he mentioned how he felt it was important that I go. I felt the weight lifted from my shoulders immediately after leaving his grave, but the monster came knocking on my door within the next few days.

The guilt came in when I felt terrible about thinking of him on the anniversary of his death instead of physically celebrating him. I contemplated so much about whether I would post him, give him a shoutout, throw a cookout, or release balloons. I battled with it so much, but the feeling of guilt forced my hand. I felt that if I showed no recognition at all, people would continue to think what they already thought from the beginning of our marriage: that I was unworthy of a decent godly man.

The amount of energy, time, and space given to guilt will surprise you if you take the time to think about where you once were, where you are now, and where you're trying to go. I believe I fought so hard for my first exclusive relationship after my husband that I was more tired from that than working a full-time job. I wanted people to believe that I deserved my husband, and I was willing to prove it by being in a relationship I had no business being in. My last relationship ended with guilt, but the difference between then and the guilt I felt before was the guilt of doing what was right and best for me.

I accepted that no matter how hard I worked, how much I changed, and how hard I tried, people would label me exactly how they wanted. This time, instead of fighting, I accepted it as what it was. Did I accept what was said to me? I accepted the fact that this person labeled me as a mistake that was made. Yes. I accepted that fact, but I didn't accept the label. Once I finally decided to choose myself and stop fighting for something that was draining me, I was everything but a child of God.

The reality of it is that I owe no one anything. I didn't owe anyone an explanation, a long paragraph of "what's" and "why's," my reasoning behind a decision I made, but I owed it to myself to release it. The saying, "Experience is the best teacher," is true. Sometimes it takes people time to go through things to understand the dynamics of a situation. What about me? I had carried this same weight around with me for 16 years, and I finally decided to release it. Guess what? I don't feel guilty at all. While thinking about your life, remember this: no amount of guilt can change the past, and no amount of anxiety can change or define the future. Choose you and I fought hard, believing I would never complete my "journey." Truth be told, the journey never ends. I am still journeying to this day. We can set goals and deadlines and even jot down what we plan to do each week or month, but your journey never ends. We are all striving daily to become better parents, spouses, and people in general. Life throws curve balls at you, and you're not always prepared for them. Sometimes when life throws one at you, it makes you feel like you have to go backwards or start all over again.

no amount of guilt can change
the past, and no amount of anxiety
can change or define the future.
Choose you, and be free.

I'd be the first to say that I've been thrown so many curve balls; I know I've started over a thousand times. I would sometimes find myself back in spaces mentally that I fought hard to get out of. I wish someone had told me ten years ago that the journey never ends. I struggled so hard to believe that I would never "cross" the finish line. The journey to complete healing, the journey to being whole, the journey of becoming a better mom, and even the journey of becoming a wife were so overwhelming to me that I would make wrong turns when I came to a four-way intersection. I would tell myself, "Okay, this month I will focus on becoming a better mom," and once I made a mental note to do that, I would be attacked emotionally and physically in another area, which distracted me.

When my husband died in 2017, I didn't turn, and I didn't go straight. I did nothing. I stopped, and I stayed there with no intention of moving. I didn't plan to stay there for a while. I made up my mind that I was not going to move at all. I had given up on a lot of things, even my children. I found myself putting them off on other people. At this time, there were only my two daughters, Aubrei and Aiyanna. During my husband's sickness, I was on a personal journey to strengthen my relationship with God. I was so young and knew nothing about marriage, but all I knew was that this man loved me. He carried me, and he covered me and my messed-up tail. He loved me for me, and he loved my children. I wanted to be better for him. I wanted to be a good wife, but I had no idea our marriage would be tested.

"Through sickness and through health," I said. Before I knew it, I had overwhelmed myself with trying to be this perfect wife to the point where I had given up mentally but was still there physically. I mean, what am I supposed to do? There I was, basically a housewife taking care of my husband. I didn't want to do it, not because I didn't love him, but because I didn't know how to. My husband was such an integral man. He would tell me to leave every single day since he was diagnosed with congestive heart failure. A part of me believed that they knew it was a lot for me and also for him too. He would tell me how hard it was on him not to be able to play around with our daughter. Believe it or not, I made a mental note to keep trying and keep going. I felt like it was the right thing to do. I made a vow to myself, to him, and to God.

I tried to cope in every single way I possibly could. I drank, I smoked. At the time, I was in a singing group, so I occupied myself with that also. I had already given up mentally. I made bad decisions. I found myself connected to the wrong people. I was doing more damage to my marriage than good, but I continued to tell myself that it didn't matter because I was still there, and I was still trying. When my husband died, it felt like my heart had stopped beating. No, literally, I felt like I had been hit by a truck and not by accident.

The people that I thought were with me became enemies. Even some of my husband's closest friends disposed of me. What shocked me the most was the fact that no one had the decency to consider my youngest daughter, our daughter. No one thought about my mental space being just a tad bit okay to be able to raise her without her father. After all, he had died three days before her birthday, and very quickly, I went from being a married mom to a widowed single mother at twenty-three. Outside of some family members, I can count on one hand who was actually there physically and even mentally for me.

After all, he had died three days before her birthday, and very quickly, I went from being a married mom to a widowed single mother at 23.

So, here I am, on the journey to complete healing, right? So, first, I thought that I needed to heal from my husband's death, but I struggled with the fact that I had specifically asked God to heal him, but he had died. I was dealing with way more than his death. The feelings of betrayal, rejection, disappointment, hurt, and guilt had all come upon me. It didn't creep up on me either. I was always angry, but I would drink myself to sleep. I'm healing though. I don't know where to start. I don't know why I'm even healing. I mean, I was so angry with God that I really didn't care about moving forward. Once I realized that I didn't care enough about myself to come out of this dark place, I used my children. I thought maybe I would heal for them. Maybe heal for Aiyanna? I wasn't sure of what to do, so I tried that, but that also didn't work. Have you ever reached the point where you have absolutely no motivation to do anything at all? I heard, "The light is at the end of the tunnel," but no one recognized that I was at the end of the tunnel, and it was still dark.

One evening, I had put the children to bed and began drinking. I figured I would just have a couple of drinks and not so many because the girls were present. One drink turned into many, and while vomiting into the toilet in the bathroom, I felt someone's hand on my back. I turned around, and I saw that it was my youngest daughter behind me. I screamed to the top of my lungs at her. I was so embarrassed. I told her to get back to bed immediately and that she had no business being up. How stupid of me not to think about my baby having to use the restroom, right? Anyway, I told her to get back to bed, and she looked at me and said she knew where a bottle of her father's old pills was. She said she would grab them for me to take so I could feel better. Her last words before I burst into tears with her in my arms were, "You have to take Daddy's medicine, so you won't get sick and go away like him."

What did the church people say? I was done. Let me be clear, I didn't motivate myself, nor did my children; life did. I wanted to live. That is when I realized that my journey had begun. I had to think of the benefits of journeying and reflect on them. Everyone's journey is different, and I was on mine then, the journey of becoming. At the time, I didn't know who I was becoming or what I was supposed to be doing, but I did know that I wanted to live, and for me to do that, I had to find out who Adrian Nelson was outside of a wife, a mother, a sister, and a friend. Just me.

To this day, I still experience good and bad days. We all do, but the decision on whether to be enslaved and bound by life and its circumstances or to be free makes your journey a little easier. I believe that every step counts, whether it be big or small. Daily, we make the same decision we made at the beginning of our journey. Our journey will have pain and failure. We should consider not only the steps forward but also the stumbles, falls, and trials along the way, the knowledge we will fail to know. Accepting that the unknown will approach us during our journey is scary, but knowing there is no destination but rather a new way of seeing during this journey will make the sacrifice much easier.

the decision on whether to be enslaved and
bound by life and its circumstances or to be
free makes your journey a little easier.

3

FREEDOM

free

adjective

1. *not subject to another's control or power; free to act or be done as one wishes*

2. not being confined or imprisoned

adverb

3. without cost or payment.

verb

4. *release* from captivity, confinement, or slavery.

I want first to say that a person is free when they have control over their own life. The psychological meaning of freedom is primarily a state of mind and not a physical condition. Freedom is important. If someone ever tells you that it isn't, they're lying. Freedom is important because it leads to an overall high quality of life. The thought of freedom, personally, was visualized as a bird flying in the sky. At least they looked free to me, but I can't help but see birds flying when I hear the word freedom. It is an overwhelming rush of excitement, anxiousness, and happiness for just a moment when you realize you are not free.

I could not tell anyone when I realized I was not free, that I had carried something from my childhood all the way up to my adulthood. I only knew that I was not free and that my methods of becoming free were all wrong. Indeed, I was born free, but I had already identified myself as a scared little girl yearning to be loved correctly. That was all I knew, and along the way, I began to continuously lose my mental freedom by identifying myself with external baggage. As I became older, memories, failures, hurts, pleasures, habits, etc., were who I had accepted myself to be, not knowing that freedom begins from within.

During the early stages of my journey towards freedom, I had to accept the fact that the things I carried were indeed undeserving, disgusting, and hurtful. I've always acknowledged that certain things have happened in my life, but I never accepted them. A friend of mine told me that although things did happen, they didn't define who I am. So, accept the fact that it happened and know that you didn't deserve it, but also flow into believing that you are not what happened. As people who have experienced traumatizing life experiences, we convince ourselves that we are undeserving of freedom. We allow these things to confine us and keep us locked in a cage, chained to our bad experiences.

Everyone wishes to be free, but no one tells us how. I can tell you now that I am currently being freed as I write this book. The cost of freedom is much more than we speak about. The feeling of guilt is the main reason why most of us are not mentally free. Once you accept what people label you, you've made the mental decision to be that very thing, and you suddenly decide that you want to be free. Chile, who do you think you are? Right? Because that's exactly what happens when you choose to be free and become a better you. No business lesson, vacation, relationship, or church service will do the work for you. You have to physically, emotionally, and mentally work towards freeing your mind from everything you've carried for however many days, months, or years.

The cost of freedom is much
more than we speak about

Making the decision to do it is in itself a struggle because you have already accepted that the external things are who you are. I made the mental decision to be completely and totally free in the year 2022. I was in the early stages of a breakup. I sat in my living room in the dark until around 3 am, crying and confused. I felt exposed and embarrassed at the fact that I was publicly declaring love and happiness within this relationship, thinking that this was it and that I would have a second chance at having a family again, but I found myself alone.

After my husband passed away, I dealt with certain individuals romantically, but this relationship was exclusive. My first exclusive relationship after my marriage failed. I cannot describe the feelings and the level of pain I was experiencing. How did I end up here? I began to think and question myself. My mind had reached a point where I could no longer hold anything mentally. I want to mention that, outside of my personal life, we were in the middle of a pandemic, which had a lot of other things that followed. That night, I made the mental decision to be free, not necessarily from this person but from myself.

I realized that I had been holding myself captive for years. Once I made that mental decision to be free, I immediately grabbed my laptop and began to type. The relief I felt just to get it out felt as if someone was lifting something that weighed maybe about 500lbs off of me. As I typed, I cried and laughed. I shook my head in disbelief that I had never gotten to the root of why I was bound and what caused me to feel that I had to accept the external. Let me tell you; I started a journey that night without even realizing that my journey towards freedom would also tie into everything I had tried to do before.

The journey to self-discovery, healing, being whole, being a good mom, etc., would tie into this journey of mine. When you decide mentally to be free, you absolutely have to move. You must physically take the first step. Do something because faith without works is dead. It can be as simple as calling out the next day from work because you need a mental break, and guess what? If they fire you or even threaten to, you can apply for another job and get it. You are in control of your own life. Accept what has happened to you. Accept your past. Make peace with these things and be free.

The next night, I slept peacefully because I knew I had fought back. I fought depression, suicidal thoughts, hurt, betrayal, loneliness, lust, alcoholism, sexual abuse, emotional abuse, mental abuse, etc. I fought against these things after the night I decided to live. Although I do feel I lost some, I fought a good fight and knew then that it was time for me to acknowledge, accept, release and be free. It is better to die fighting for freedom than to die a prisoner, whether that's physically or mentally.

It is better to die fighting for freedom than to die a prisoner, whether that's physically or mentally.

4

MISHANDLED

mishandled

transitive verb.

1. managed or dealt with (something) wrongly or ineffectively.
2. rough or careless manipulation

I want to piggyback on the chapter "INNOCENCE" for a second. Taking the innocence of another person could be the most manipulative and painful feeling ever experienced by the victim. Know that when this is being done, there are multiple ways you can snatch something away from a person. Whether it's done intentionally or subtly, you can take away a person's peace, motivation, joy, take advantage of another's body, etc. (if the person lets you). But, there's one feeling that is most commonly known, especially among women, that is most commonly used for beneficial reasons: "The Snatcher."

Being vulnerable personally is the scariest feeling to have as a woman. Nowadays, we suppress our hurt to avoid being mishandled during our vulnerable moments. I've had the "tossed around" experience multiple times. Some of those times I could control, while during the other times, I could not or had given up on fighting the emotions that come with being mishandled. Feeling used, neglected, and unworthy all at once was something I had carried with me since childhood, and because I carried these feelings, I found myself looking for love in all the wrong places.

Once I began to confide in certain individuals, one particularly "The Narcissist," I realized that not only had I been mishandled, but I also realized I had been mishandled quite a few times in different situations. When I speak of mishandling, I am not speaking of things we have brought upon ourselves. Accountability leads to healing and acceptance. Being mishandled when you are absolutely undeserving is another thing that ties into being innocent. You have to teach people how to treat you. Most people only want to be connected with others who are already living whole and free. I will not discredit the people that have no time to "teach" anyone.

Sometimes, we think of this saying with a closed mindset. Teaching someone how to treat you requires you to set boundaries for yourself. Setting boundaries and practicing them gives others no room to try you twice. People will mishandle you, toss you around, and mistreat you, but when boundaries are set, it won't happen again, whether it's the same person or another. It's unfortunate that I had to learn this the hard way, but it's better late than never. Being used for the benefit of other people and allowing it not only made me realize that I had become accustomed to this type of love language, but I also lacked the understanding of how hurt the people hurting me were.

Now, that is no excuse, nor is it okay for anyone to abuse you in any way due to their past traumas and experiences, but it goes beyond us as individuals. Personally, it is extremely important for everyone now and in the near future to be connected to me divinely. Not only have my past traumatic experiences forced me to grow mentally faster than I was supposed to, but they also showed me that it's okay to have connections that are beneficial to me and the other party in a healthy way — being mishandled personally caused me to operate in pain for many years. I didn't realize that being treated undeservingly horribly had me subtly do the same thing to other people.

I didn't realize that being treated undeservingly horribly had me subtly do the same thing to other people.

Although I am still learning and growing mentally, there are many things I wish I could've done differently, but I'm grateful to have another chance to give people the raw and authentic me now. It all goes from me making the decision to forgive the ones who had hurt me, forgiving myself for accepting whatever was handed to me, and being able to operate in love and freedom. Your greatest test will be how you handle people who mishandle you. Learning not to take everything personally was a huge thing I had to learn. I wasn't interested in why a person did something to me. I'm not a therapist, nor am I God. The only thing that concerned me was the thing that had happened.

Currently, moving in freedom has taught me things about myself I never knew. I am choosing not to be mishandled again. You literally sit and think about the things you take personally at work, at home, and in the outside world, and sometimes you find yourself shaking your head and asking yourself why. Instead of brushing it off and saying, "It won't happen again," really take some time to answer the question you've asked yourself. All I ever wanted was effort, and I was after the type of treatment I felt like I deserved, so I gave time, patience, love, and energy to things that felt like situational hell.

I was trying to be good enough for people who were comfortable with mishandling me and my heart. Once you reach your "edge," you are at a crossroads. You can either make the decision to suppress your feelings and ignore your edge, or you can decide to jump. The overwhelming rushing of the wind that your body feels, similar to a rollercoaster ride, naturally makes your body brace itself for whatever is next. I jumped, and I braced myself for the landing, not knowing if I would fall to my death or if I would land safely.

There are many times we feel like we won't accept something again or decide we won't tolerate a specific thing or person any longer. Everyone reaches a breaking point, and most of the time, that is what it takes for people to make a life-changing decision. I landed hard but safely, and then I got up. Although I stood with marks and bruises, I put my feet in the right place and stood firmly. Looking at the marks, the bruises, the hurt and turmoil I had battled with for years... looking at me. It was a bittersweet moment. The truth is, the scars will always be there as a reminder of what I have been through and how hard I fought to get through those situations.

The fact that I was still here and standing strong was the most refreshing feeling of it all as I looked in the mirror. The strength I felt after realizing it did not come from me feeling as if I had won but from me deciding to be free mentally. That is what makes me strong, choosing to take the first step towards freedom. Confidently walking in the power of knowing that you control your happiness, your life, and your freedom is a different kind of power. Take care of yourself first and foremost because the minute you decide not to, you become unbalanced, and before you know it, you will end up mishandling yourself and others. Whenever you feel compelled to put others first at your expense, you deny your own reality, your identity. Choose to forgive, choose to be free. Choose you.

Whenever you feel compelled to put others first at your expense, you deny your own reality, your identity.

5

PREPARATION/ QUALIFICATION

Many people are living without guidance or motivation even to begin to know why they are living. Some people have lived and gone through many things and have decided to turn their life events into something positive. Others have realized their purpose without having to go through anything at all. Everyone has their own story, journey, and testimony as to why they do the things they do. In order to prepare for what you're meant to do, many people feel like they aren't qualified to do it. First of all, I want to say that your purpose qualifies you. Everything doesn't come from a degree in school. Experience also qualifies you. I spent many seasons believing that I needed a degree to fully operate in my purpose, and while I may or may not decide to pursue a degree in the future, I am qualified to flow in my purpose right now.

I had experienced many years of having ideas and wanting to go after a particular thing or achieve specific goals, but I felt unqualified to do them, and the guilt that followed behind me had always found its way in front of me. I felt like I had to be "perfect for the job," and because of that, I held myself hostage. I had not put a pause but a stop to even having the thought of pursuing my goals. I would start a thing and never finish it, or I'd have a thought, write it down, but end up throwing it away or not prioritizing the actions I needed to take to pursue those goals.

There really isn't much you can tell a person to do but to just DO IT. I will be the first to say that deciding to just go and work with what you have will have you feeling like you can literally accomplish any and every goal you have set for yourself. Personally, I overwhelmed myself mentally with all these ideas, and I ended up not doing anything at all. Something I have learned the hard way is to not have a plan B. It is better to be prepared for whatever comes next. After all, being in the unknown on your own is scary, but knowing that you want to do something and knowing that it will absolutely work this time is an even better feeling.

I decided to go after my goals, and that was it. I stopped allowing myself to think that if this didn't work, I'd try something else. No, this is going to work, and once I have completed this, I will move forward to my next goal. See, we are all different, and we all do things differently. Some people can juggle multiple things at once, which I believe is a great quality to have, but it takes lots of patience and practice. But what led me to believe that having a plan B wasn't an option for me was the fact that I was always starting something and not finishing it. Or, I would start something and move on to something else, forgetting in the middle of it that I had to go back to finish the first thing I had stated.

No, this is going to work, and once I have completed this, I will move forward to my next goal.

All this time, I was literally all over the place, and my mind was so overwhelmed with the fact that maybe this just wasn't for me because if it was, I wouldn't be going through this. I am not qualified for this. I'm not prepared for this. So, I gave up many times, feeling unprepared and unqualified. If you change the way you look at things, the things you look at will change. Perhaps when you thought you weren't good enough for the job, the truth was you were overqualified. Convince yourself beyond a shadow of a doubt that you are prepared and qualified for the course, the dream job, your new business, and so on. "You are the artist of your own life; don't hand the paintbrush to someone else."

"You are the artist of your own life; don't hand the paintbrush to someone else."

6

STAGNATION

stagnation

noun

1. The state of not flowing or moving
2. Lack of activity, growth or development

Stagnation often comes because some people believe there isn't anything that excites or motivates them enough to take action. First, if you don't have the habit of even setting goals but instead visualize them without taking any action toward them, you're experiencing stagnation. Personally, I experienced symptoms of stagnation for many years. It wasn't the fact that it felt like I couldn't do it, but I would always somehow make everything else more important than my goals. I guess I felt like I had enough time to pursue my goals anytime I wanted to.

Another critical reason stagnation had taken control of my life was the fact that I had become lazy. It's hard to admit certain things about yourself, considering that you are getting up daily and actually doing what needs to be done, but speaking of my goals and dreams? I had become lazy. The truth is, I never permitted myself to push a little harder. I had become content with working, caring for the home and the children, and just going with the flow. It was only a few months ago when I made the mental decision to move, which leads me back to say that I genuinely believe that everyone has to reach some point in their life that forces them to move. It could be death, a failed relationship, financial problems, etc.

I genuinely believe that everyone has to reach some point in their life that forces them to move.

I struggled so much yearning for connections with individuals, believing that if I just had someone who could relate to the way, I felt, maybe that'd comfort the feeling of stagnation I'd been experiencing. It's mind-boggling to me that there are so many "self-help" books and events, so many women and men empowerment motivational speakers and influencers I've read and been connected to but always feel the same a day or two later. I always felt like I had to turn my pain into purpose until I changed my perspective on that saying. I didn't want to change my pain into anything; I just wanted it to be gone.

I didn't want to change my pain into anything; I just wanted it to be gone.

I realized that I needed to release some things in order for me to not only flow but flow freely. Everyone doesn't process things the same way. The look or feeling of freedom is different for everyone, so no matter how many books I read, how many events I went to, and how many people tried to push me towards my goals, I hadn't given myself permission to move. I realized no one would do it for me. We often find ourselves hoping for a great big miracle to happen out of nowhere. Faith without works is dead. You have to move. You have to decide what your next move will be.

Being stagnant not only hinders you from pursuing your goals but also from living your day-to-day life. I formed the habit of only living but not living free. I was moving every day, but I wasn't moving forward or backward. I was stuck. Years and years have passed since I was still in the same spot. I did make an effort to launch my image consulting business in 2021, but that was all I did. I launched, and I stayed there. A friend of mine made an effort to utilize my services by including me in a Mother's Day Makeover to push me. Although I had recently found out about my pregnancy, I still did what I was supposed to do. That day was the best I had had in a very long time. Here I was operating on something I wanted to do, and it flowed effortlessly through me. I was called to do this thing, and maybe that day was a "test drive" for me. I'll never know why God allowed me to be able to provide my services that day, but I'm glad it happened the way it did.

I never did anything else after that, but instead, I stared at the pictures that were taken almost every day and wondered how far I could take this thing or maybe if I could do it again. The actions behind my thoughts weren't aligned either. I didn't realize I was stuck until I realized I was stuck, and man, that wasn't a good feeling. Not only did I realize I was stuck, but I also realized I had been stuck for years. Stagnation is death. It's dark, and it's consuming. If you don't move, if you don't take action, you wither away mentally, physically, emotionally, and spiritually and eventually die. It's that simple; it's that scary. MOVE!

"The first step towards getting somewhere is to first decide you aren't going to stay where you are." — John Piermont "J.P" Morgan

7

ELEVATION

You cannot be in a relationship without a purpose. Submission comes with the mission. The elevation that came along with my healing process had mentally elevated me, which then allowed me to put things into action at home.

Submission comes with the mission.

"Our mission as a family is to live a life of honesty, integrity, and unconditional love." to never lose sight of what's important. We will inspire others with our actions by following the example God has set for us. Giving before receiving, never fearing mistakes, and honoring our commitments. We will be physically, spiritually, mentally, and financially healthy. We will be present in the moment while changing lives, one person at a time. We will submit to the vision of our protector (husband), honoring God while following our leader (head of household) in the assurance that he will lead us to greatness. We will submit to the mission, keeping God first in everything we do. **By honoring God first by submitting to him and his word, I will eat better, live better, walk better, and talk better. I will be better. I will be the best** You cannot be in a relationship without a purpose. Submission comes with the mission. The elevation that came along with my healing process had mentally elevated me, which then allowed me to put things into action at home.

"Our mission as a family is to live a life of honesty, integrity, and unconditional love." to never lose sight of what's important. We will inspire others with our actions by following the example God has set for us. Giving before receiving, never fearing mistakes, and honoring our commitments. We will be physically, spiritually, mentally, and financially healthy. We will be present in the moment while changing lives, one person at a time. We will submit to the vision of our protector (husband), honoring God while following our leader (head of household) in the assurance that he will lead us to greatness. We will submit to the mission, keeping God first in everything we do. **By honoring God first by submitting to him and his word, I will eat better, live better, walk better, and talk better. I will be better. I will be the best mother I can possibly be to Aubrei and Aiyanna. I will continue to focus on walking into my purpose and pursuing my career, goals, and dreams. "Going hard" with elegance and grace.**

I am a Queen. The world may be reluctant to see my crown, but God is ever so accepting of me. I was automatically deemed royalty as a child of God. I was born with royal blood. I am crowned with glory and honor; I have dominion over all. No official title is needed other than "child of the Creator of the universe." My right to the throne isn't just happenstance. I am God's chosen treasure. He called me out of a very dark place to experience the light, and claimed me as his own. "

I was automatically deemed
royalty as a child of God

"When everything's wrong and broken, instead of harping on what's wrong and broken, find what works and build on that."

8

MISHANDLED PROPERLY

I refuse to allow my past traumas, past mistakes, and the opinions of others to lead me into self-sabotaging the freedom of self-love, genuine love, happiness, divine connection, and the blessings God has for me.

"I am accountable."

"I am forgiven."

"I am loved."

"I am free."

The truth of the matter is, no matter how bad your life may have seemed to be up till now, we are all here on purpose.

`Even after all of this, don't spend a lot of time worrying and appreciate what is present right now. Own your story, own your truth. It's okay to "feel." You don't always have to "thug it out," but remember that emotions could sometimes be valid, but most times, they're incorrect and in-factual. The truth of the matter is, no matter how bad your life may have seemed to be up till now, we are all here on purpose. But wait, how can someone mishandle you properly? It's simple. Every single thing that was set out to destroy you actually built you.

Every single thing that was set out to destroy you actually built you.

I always think of the way people mishandled me growing up and even now in my adult years, and I'm rushed with a sense of gratitude. I haven't always felt this way. I used to become extremely angry and even disappointed in myself, but honestly and indeed, I am thankful. I would not be the woman I am today if my life hadn't taken me down several different roads. I used to always think I had to have some sort of public stand to share my truth and my story, but I realized there had to be a moment of relief. I am not degreed, I am not popular or have multiple businesses (yet), but I am simply blessed. I am healed, and I am whole. For this, I feel like I have already won.

> *I would not be the woman I am today if my life hadn't taken me down several different roads.*

I have to thank God for allowing certain things to go the way they did. Yes, I was mishandled, but there was nothing more the enemy or my enemies could do outside of what was already done. Writing this with a sense of gratitude only makes me realize that I've grown in different areas in my life. I wouldn't say I liked the things that were done to me, said about me, and even the things I used upon myself on my own, but I am thankful for the way those things molded me into what and who I am today. It notably challenged me personally but has been beneficial throughout my family and my personal home.

> *Yes, I was mishandled, but there was nothing more the enemy or my enemies could do outside of what was already done.*

The scariest thing I've encountered was being able to be a mother. Not a "good" mother but one in general. I lived in fear for most of my life, and once my firstborn entered this world, I immediately began to fear that she would go through the things that I did. As a mom, now, I am open to love. I am open to hearing the emotion and thoughts of my children without feeling any doubt about me not being a good parent; I am free internally. No one mishandled me; they simply handled me the way they were supposed to, and being mishandled, I am now a changed woman.

There are so many great things in store for me, for my business, Mishandled Properly. Come to think about it, I launched this business in 2021, not knowing what came with it, not even realizing I wasn't prepared for everything that came with my purpose. There I launched with a little one growing inside of me, and I didn't even know. I've used every single last thing, good and bad, and turned it into something greater than myself. I've changed the direction of my focus.

We have to understand that there's no such thing as "keeping up" with anyone else. We are all doing this thing as individuals. I always felt left behind, but truth be told, I am right on track. I'm very particular about what I share with people and what advice I give to some, but passionately, I will say that you are on your own journey. Don't ever feel like you're moving too fast or slow, especially regarding your healing process. Take all the time you need. We are all flawed, and everyone is battling with something. Use your disadvantages to your advantage. Use your pain for your purpose.

Everything that happens with or to us isn't always beautiful but knowing that we are here on purpose and with a purpose is more than enough advice to keep going. This isn't a self-help book or a 30-day challenge for you but simply my truth, my story (partially). I am taking full ownership of Adrian, and no one can take this away from me, for I was and am Mishandled Properly.

ABOUT THE AUTHOR

Adrian Nelson is just a country girl born in Hartsville, South Carolina, and raised in High Point, North Carolina. She is the mother of two girls and one boy. She experienced the loss of her belated husband, Ayendai Evans, in the year of 2017 and relocated to Winston Salem, NC. Adrian launched an Image Consulting business in the year of 2019. She is now pursuing her degree in an effort to maintain a successful yet effective business that will not only empower women to face their challenges headstrong but to also give women the opportunity to embrace who they are inside. She received her Image Consulting certificate in August of 2020.

NOTES

NOTES

Made in the USA
Middletown, DE
12 February 2023